Earshot

Earshot

Sam Morley

PUNCHER & WATTMANN

First published in 2022
Published by Puncher & Wattmann
PO Box 279
Waratah NSW 2298

info@puncherandwattmann.com

NATIONAL
LIBRARY
OF AUSTRALIA

A catologue record for this book is available from The National Library of Australia.

ISBN   9781922571441

Cover design by David Musgrave

Printed by Lightning Source International

To Zoe for quietly believing in me
and to Hugo and Reuben
for giving me something quiet to believe in

Your exact errors make a music
that nobody hears
—William Stafford

It's so delicate, the light.
And there's so little of it
—Rolf Jacobsen

Contents

A dream track to sleep

Verandah

As the sun simmered
my father watched the last light
lap onto the verandah.
He hissed through his cigarette
teeth yellowing in his slack gums.
By then death had reached him.

When he was buried
I just stood there boy squinting
between men in town hats and tweed
who were mute when words
may have made flesh a memory
now only sashed in smoke.

Family lounge

Summer smeared us across
the stale hours of a test match.
Outside if you took a mower
to the dry grass it would fire.

So mostly we were here
in the pleasant gloom
under the ceiling stains
those ink blooms, light

at right angles
slicing the doily blinds
asterixing dust along a line
from deep fine leg to mid off.

Deployed

The day the parachuter landed
summer grass whispered at his knees
way out in the back corner of the paddock
where we knew brown snakes lived.

His parachute would have followed him
a slow silk dome folding grace
and in the split second after landing
he was a child again under falling bedsheets.

We bunched two steps behind as mum
stood hand on hip, talking to this silhouette
this fly wire jet fighter who saw districts
ahead and could stride three fields long.

By then his veins had stopped shuddering
he'd packed his collection of sky into a bag
the plummeting youth of the day was gone and
all he wanted was to find a way back home.

Abattoir song

the shuffle hooves
click head-to-hide cattle
the press of mud-shit
billiard eyes shunt
grunting low beams
of steaming semis

under mire ratchet
of gurking yards
herd of udders hassled
down iron chutes
by breathless kelpies
not needing to bark

as a child I hear all this
a dream track to sleep
across damp paddocks
slaughter lights and cleavers
the sluice of filling throats
and death sheds wintering

Backseat driving

on the carpet at the rear of the family car
juddering engine our throats to the night sky
with mum green in the face from the dash
light long roads thrum bodies still heads
flung in stone whiplash the skirts of trees
sway left then right nothing lurid in the arbour
the bulk of our skulls tom-peeping at cauliflower
blooms of eucalypt swelling and trailing leaf calligraphy
stars clicked on and wincing at how trees
flare like a hall being passed through

Mail order

The old men's hair styles are the same —
parted partway from the temple
curling silver grey blonde
wave slick with Brylcreem.

The cancer skin of these men
flushes pink in the Filipina bars
old and flaming, shirts open like
Miami-Hollywood-Down Under Man.

They say it's too early for the barongs.
That you *pull that shit in the villages*
where the girls are young and dumb
cos those pineapple clothes will kill ya.

In the hotels, we see them —
lazy ugly popped out guts cackling
about *little brown fucking machines.*
And the women get pushed from behind

by families in nipper huts in provinces
and barrio rubbish mounds.
They say *Hey Joe, guapo guapo*
as the men smile stupid stupid with San Miguel

and show off square wallets fat with pesos
and photos of Mercedes with the top down
and caravans on the edge of the bush.
The women practise saying *woop woop*

the men say *we've had enough rice to be Chinese*
and they say *come back with me sweety*
and see my fast car for fast women
as their arms lump over them like damp.

Long run with a stray Staffy

Wherever it was you had come from
you didn't demand a thing. For each running step
of mine you laid the four prints of your being.

The flaked road towed us
through the Wimmera hills hunched as dunes
your paws sank deep with each stride.

And I didn't owe a thing
to your lockjaw brawn and box head
but the unending road running on before us

would have scrambled every simple synapse
of your homeless mind now unmapped outside
the bouquet of urine and last night's camp.

You hung on with a croupy cough
and goosestep turning the cold winds
warm with a discordant staccato.

How could I ever account for this meeting
of the unmoored now halfway
through a route on a day almost done.

When we turned for home the old savant
in you knew it, the spittle blow
thread traces calling for reprieve.

We found our rhythm
where your smallness was of equal weight
in the brief intimacy of our breath.

Your weeping eyes had learnt the art of loyalty
and with your range met you unleashed
that tongue sprawl and took off again.

Walking with my father in law

The bull stands square and stares.
Its shadow slinks through electric wires

follows us past the old gums
torqued out of the paddock.

We cross the creek, listen
for its ground thump.

Ants unsnarl under our feet.
A hare snatches the horizon.

He asks if I am ready to be a father.
The bull slides up, says *I think so.*

All he replies is *keep it simple.*
I thunk a stone into the creek.

Its head drops
as the water moves endlessly on.

Middle distance

A thin mist gauzes the night
fifty metres above track work.
I join the running squad late
a last minute supplicant at the back.

The runners steam
spirits shimmying
above shoulders finding
a cadence that burns.

Sports lights cascade
a mountain of hissing darkness
as bodies bounce around the track
orbiting flares of sweat and speed.

From afar we travel silently
like magi that slip between shadows.
I follow the next runner in good faith
each exhalation an attempt at communion.

A faraway moon spills
over tiled roofs and cut grass.
All around life lives on without us
a city sleeps, streetlights blur loose

applause for every pace we make
around this 400 metre loop that only
ever reaches where we began.
We press on

each falter of our heartbeats
counting down the bends.
I grope for air like a face from a Goya
and wonder how the dead saints

on all those church walls
are always painted wrong with
long necks and wide eyes
to look up with grace at God.

But what matters now is making
the next line in my lane, each step
a summons to endure and keep enduring
as the night gets longer and pulls away.

And through the slack claps and coach cries
all I can do is front straight ahead
hope each breath lasts, stride as if
this momentum means something.

The sound of the moon

and its barefoot choir
descends onto an empty field
ringing a bowl, pouring out sorrow.

Go on, step down here
be among the shadow scrawl.
From the end of the hall

a fiddle bows long notes
and the moon doles out songs
pleading with me to be still

to listen to its crushed linen
to trace the outline of its lesions.
But I sit and wait as time

ticks on an eBay auction
quickening the minutes into seconds.
Outside the stars join in too

those hopeful far-off pebbles
tuning their fibres to a frequency
now lost on a man online.

Skating at 40

Choose the surest foot
the one you start a race with
the one that leads on ice
the one to take you into the world again

The ground moves faster now
leaning forward, lurching back
the place you knew skids into shins
leaving bone shards of loose bearings

Stand up for a moment
never ahead of yourself
lean into the tilt of the earth
this path prefers you frozen

Find ballast
in the balls of your sailor's feet
still searching for the still point
on this concrete sea

Ibis

we always cycled
the light craning across
cut cloth paddocks
that eggnog milk
dusking the grass harvest

tick tick clunk
derailleur rust
a copper dust
that fell on silent roads
we knew never went

anywhere
now an ibis picks through
the neighbour's yard
formica black bill
bent tines of a suburb

tiptoeing over Macca's bags
Coke Zeros
a city of bin scab birds
the ibis says
it's been a mistake to stay here

time now to go
I promise I'll be buried
in that light again
where we ride the sunsets
that lean into our eyes

What counts for
silence here

Closing time

I am closing my eyes, because I can't see in the dusk
the poem that is already there.

I am hearing the closing time bickering of noisy mynas
and I am getting messages from the magpies tuning up.

I am hoping I can learn something from the storm clouds
content for now to veil the lavender moon.

Am I cheating the woman who laps her head across my legs?
Your gaze is distant from the morning sickness and the fear.

I palm your hair and find one, then two, then a third grey hair
and I feel weary like my life just got added to yours.

And I wonder if you're thinking about how our lives will change.
But you aren't — you are hoping the new lemon tree will grow.

Perfection only deals in moments
and for a perfect moment

I can slouch as slow as storm clouds and stand
my ground like the sapling outside our window.

Or else go mad, spinning and clicking
like cicadas do to welcome the dark.

Toboggan

We launch feet first
bodies balled
your cheek cupped
against my back.
Legs spread
the spray slaps us
running rivulets into
the private grooves
of the inner thigh.

Above our frantic
shushing the sky
stays quiet.
I want you to burrow
into my body breathe
your whole being into me
and watch it bounce apart.
Everywhere silver coins
are tossed into sunlight.

It's a balance of sorts
you know just how
to right our tilt
before we end up
limbs in the grass.
Later when we are done
when snow turns to mud
you look to me and say
we can't stop this now.

Green

You asked if I was tired from the long day
when we walked from one river mouth
to another along a wind-clapped coast.

By 5.30 your eyes were closed and each breath
deepened into the next, one, then another
meeting the low murmur of the sea.

When evening flanked the caravan
hidden in our beachside scrub
you slept as everything around got greener.

The angled branches darkened
grass thickened its soft crush hands
hunchback trees crowded the ground.

Every bit of shrub grew muscular
pressing down starlings flying home
under the ebbing arms of tea-tree.

I hoped that you would see all this
perhaps take it as some sign
for the child growing within you.

But you just turned over
curving away from the onshore winds
making a private bay from the cold.

Estuary

Seagulls escort pelicans to sea
emissaries sent out above the river mouth
to embark an armada of sails.

Further out, waves fold over themselves
a threadbare link between the crinkle
of black ocean and sky.

The breakers chomp at children
who skittle on sand that atomises
into a thousand lightweight lips.

We wonder how hard it is to know
where things join, where salt in the sea
becomes tannin in the stream

while in the eddy of our embrace we walk
slowly, noting the effervescence at our feet
and the loose lines we've left behind.

Finding you

Neon lights poke bedroom curtains
and fingers cease to be fingers
no longer mute extensions
but short range sensors sparking
the green of our bodies

A whole arm can be electrocution
shuddering pale-blue light
the numb hum of current
on the backside of your knee
the feel of silk on the thumb

If the body wasn't here
we'd be gypsy maestros
diviners of some quiet magic
parting grooves in the air
hearing song where there is none

Switching across the contours
of skin creeps daylight
showing a swell of shoulder
and the aimless rise and fall
of the pressing on flesh

It begins and ends here
a stationary journey
the warm gather of sheets
above a dreamer in the bed
an intuition of what's next

Black Saturday

1. During

when we arrived the north wind
flung gravel through trees
grass seethed at a blood clot sun

smoke stole back clouds
burnished everything in rage
a nightmare halo

we had come for the waterhole
to slip through that green sleeve
but fire howled in its rose cathedral

an asphyxiated dome groped for air
ash went after songless birds
and we gulped in the petrifying world

2. After

through a groove in the grass
flattened by rain

there is just enough of an opening
to see the scalp of the land

is still flaking
the grass bends

beneath the weight of water
a hoop genuflection

a soaked weave
impossible to pass

after the storm
when insects lace

fluted columns
and bars of sunshine

the mynas return, urchins
that never stand on ceremony

Outside on a winter night

Mist brushes skin left bare.
A million moths kissing
like no lover ever could.

I move my head as an owl
and wait with a long regard listening
to the street's stop move stop.

The neighbourhood Rottweilers flare
and the commission flat's strip lighting
pulses a dashed Morse code

across a snarl of hard rubbish.
A police helicopter heat maps
the creek for runaways.

What counts for silence here
is cut open by masked lapwings
sirening straight lines home.

In our lounge room
lamplight domes my love
and all her unread books.

Each turning page shushes now
a sieve of loose rain
a fog between here and there.

I remember spring a decade ago
when we flat backed ourselves
on an afternoon dwarfed by clouds

calling out the contours of the sky
following each clean-cut cumulus
until it blended inevitably with another.

Every few months

the lemon-scented gum
finds more muscle
thickens its young bones.
Every time it does this

I prune its branches
from everything
I have built beneath it.
It is a problem to have

a lemon-scented gum
next to the fence
and the neighbour
a charge hangs over all.

New boughs keep nodding
toward our home.
Some choices
never really leave us

they just darken
like a stone in winter.
I have found ways to wait
but the thing keeps growing

elongating every dusk
a western sun
burning along its limbs
a little longer each day.

The nature strip cut

a gash in the green
plume and red entrails
a spill of cartilage
rubber bone and one
last searching kiss

Succulent open mouth
the lost bloom of blood
eyes that would have once
dilated like a lover laughing
in the early winey days

An areole after sucking
going sticky in the sun
and the maw gone quiet
under hovering breath
and the crest of surging air

Cold as cut watermelon
in the tick whips of summer
when lips were wet
and the salty lick of pink
burnt holes in the flesh

Chest open to the sky
the last flight leaves
a milky way of feathers
with its frail grasp on grass
its dispersal of fabric fading away

She is in there somewhere, showering

It was that morning
she was in there showering
that I thought I saw the woman
I hadn't seen for years

The tendons of her feet
the finest mechanisms of tension
the smooth groove of her back
the place where our water had once run

As I watched she said nothing
but rather gathered up her body
as if she had dropped
a bag of apples in the market

It was there between the shift of steam
and the siren of children
I listened harder than ever
to the sound of running water again

As we lay in bed

I was thinking how dark it was
so dark in that room
as outside the bruised moon
struggled to draw
shadows from trees.

I wish I could say I took you
that our limbs looped
that our thoughts never cut
the coppice of our bodies
but the night didn't go like that.

Overhead, the planes moaned
as the sheets between us
got colder and unsettled
and the dark got pitch
and never let us sleep.

Wimmera

escarpment prints
parchment for the dawn

states a claim that
it made this place laid out

the scrub from the waist down
and began the new morning

we believe this only partly
down here in the valley

the earth still sleeps in
shallows of night black

gowns over banksia
grass trees shrugging dreams

we always start like this
hand in hand

until the first incline
then a slow separation begins

*

we failed the first test of walking
which is to let the path bind you

early winds tilt into whipsticks
shattering the crows

in the low scrim of sclerophyll
you think it is all for all

*

yesterday we swerved the car in vain
from the slate tiles of a shingleback

its insides spread like a bloodied hankie
today the lizard is resurrected

a small skink *god* snagged
on thirst opening and shutting

it's quiet clam mouth
as light chafes the valley

and a southerly slaps
the sandstone into place

*

kangaroos judicial and upright
stare out to the plains

and the *eek eek*
of charred trees after fire

across drought acres they
smell rain so fine

it will die before it arrives
we should have moved together

found the horses in their wild faces
watched harp-string hinds snap

past the fly-drenched stump
of some dead animal and its simmering spine

*

by mid-morning the moon has
cut off half of its life

shedding a shoulder to hold the day
for each white fist of cloud there

is a corrugated arm
crumpled and unlit

sand burrs in my boots
gnawing skin into blood

and all of it rising and rising
the mountain range within

Kelp

Unravelling on the beach
hides darkening in the sun
are the bodies of a forest
whose foliage once slipped in
spokes of underwater light.

In the water's sunspill they flared
braids straddled over the seabed
one pulse above a barren floor —
a surging lung, the shifting mane
of a far-flung shelf of life.

Then one day it all unhitched.
The sea loosened its wide belts
tossing cut cloth ashore
and when it cast out love it was
with entrails open, crisping at our feet.

A hinge opening on a home

Black lake

The steering is slack until you crank
the gurgling outboard motor.

We push past the last buoy
and I find myself standing.

Over open water, air circles
the blackness underneath.

I pull my children closer.
Cormorants dive, find nothing

and rise as oily shadows up a wall.
I cut the engine and we slide

slowly on the skin of the lake —
chiaroscuro in a graphite field.

Water mounds, then wears away.
The children scuttle and chiack.

I feel something slick, a vague
threat closing, a regret I can't repair.

On the expanding cross-hatch of lead
I watch an accumulation of shapes

contours of nothing that do not remain
long enough to define themselves.

Week 20 ultrasound

The first time I hear you
you are grainy notes
on your own distant moon
loud among the dust
and grey sediment of
the lonely planet you are

Where you are living
you cannot hear me among
the alien deities of your land
the powdery cordilleras
pulsing with the winds
composed by velvet wings

Right now all you are
is a tin sheet shaken by storms
a windmill straining to hold
its clatter-bones together
under the canter of a gale
eager to move further on

But one day you will lengthen
that thinning cloth shape
into hands and will make fists
because I have spoken
the final word on a matter
and you'll say I am not listening

Humpback (Pacific)

I make my boys stand in the wind
and look at the ocean
unhinging itself over and over.

I tell them that among the waves
there is a mass of blue permanence
that below the surface tension of water

there are escapees from our squinting.
I tell them to wait for their bodies to break
the susurrating gossip of the sea.

Then, punching vapour over the rail
of the wavering horizon
filament fists scatter in the offshore breeze.

We see their slick nodes heading south
sounding sinus clicks
lobtailing their flukes like petals.

I point to the whales clapping the drum of the world.
But all my children can say is we're cold
and ask when we can go back inside.

Gold laced Wyandotte

You were once a noon sun
blazing through the roost.
Now you lie like a loosely
bound bag of gold.

Your rouge comb has paled
the wattle has whitened.
Every gold laced feather has curled
a hundred spangled sunsets

folding to the dirt.
A reappearing apparition
at shallow bowls of turned earth.
Now homeless in your own home

the flock has forgotten the dying.
The hock hangs
as rigor mortis stands by
stiffening the hours.

When the evening comes
children cry in secret for you
asking to spare that final blow.
They know a hole is dug for morning.

Mud

At the creek's flood plain
of rock still sleek
from three days of rain
my sons sink in silt banks
suddenly heavy and big.
Stooping at every black pool
flinging sludge from rock scallops
they smooth the grainy basalt
down their arms.
Wafting toward their soft heat
mid-flight mosquitos hang
their fine-laced legs
smelling blood beneath
earth-enamelled flesh.
One son appears at my side
waiting for his new skin to dry.
He watches the dark slick shatter
a grey casing encrusting him
in a promise paper-thin.

Treehouse

Sometimes he'll climb down
to his fire, shovel mulch and sand
and dead things and cook it in his oven.
I'll say *watch for spiders* but it's always
too late. He's moved back up
heaving his bucket of bracken to fill it
from a tap with no water only light.
Then he climbs higher beyond his home
stepping up new branches that arc
beneath his feather bones.
He is looking beyond the passing planes
to where the sky turns to blue dots
in his eyes. I hope he cannot hear me
call out warnings, because I made this house
for him, this jerry-built tangle of timber
that I should have always known
he'd find his way out of.

My sons watch the storm

as it spurs itself over open country
a hooded beast looking up from a field away
then widening its stride toward us.

The wind gathers in its arms all
the most frightening moments of our lives
throws them at us and wails.

We pull close, zip our coats.
An anvil of cloud slams the small herd of trees
with slanting grains of rain and mica flares

fasten to the earth, the world
in momentary seizure. Our heads hung
the storm rushes us up the hill.

A catacomb closes over. Even children know
when the day is split, when the weather within us
changes, when something final has arrived.

Christmas

I am in the shed sweeping
when my neighbour knocks at the front door
and tells my partner her husband is cheating.

She says he just rolled up his swag
on 40 years of marriage and throttled
his new motorbike to who knows where.

At the same time my two boys are nearby
painting sunsets, when I ask them if
they think the world could last forever.

One says *no*
it is most definitely scientifical
there will be big flames, we are too close to the sun.

The other says *yes, forever*
because he thinks that just thinking
the word forever is enough.

The youngest boy then says he wants to paint
a golden tombstone for one of our chooks
that died the week before. To him death

isn't anything other than the colour of life.
In that week of dying they cry every time
I pick up a shovel or speak with a solemnity

that makes them think I have God within me.
But my children don't understand God yet
or the idea of it or how it can draw a line

between now and the hereafter. And I don't
want them to know the divine or a heaven.
What I want is for them to know there is a line.

If I'd known, I'd have taken them to the front door
to meet my neighbour and her Christmas cheer
got them to thank her for her sparkling gifts.

I'd have made them listen to the smallest sounds
that came from her as she pushed up her glasses
to look at the tinsel festooned on the porch.

And I'd have trained them to find the slightest
mercy mixed in the low simmer of dusk.
But it never went like that – my neighbor

just waved it off and my boys became
quiet as if a constellation of dust motes
had burned and died around them.

High ropes

Climbing to the top
of a four metre mountain
of steel and sailors' rope
my son at the apex
of his seven years decides
it is now time to show
this younger generation
what living really is.
Tipping his world over
he flips to point his soft
skull to the ground feet
hooked over a bar.
Charged with voices saying
he is capable of flying today
his hands come free
as the prospect looms
that the earth will meet him
at 9.8 metres per second
per second and though
covered in tan bark
it will still surely drag
down what it can get.
The younger kids watch
as they do when seeing
fireworks and they duly
check to see if their mums
have something to say
about all this.
From my distance finally
I call out and my boy comes
again to the right angles
this world requires

and he says *what?*
smiling and silent
at the same time.

To sleep in a strange place

1.
in a corner of the dark
he paces lickety-split
arms stiff to his sides
hands flat out fidgeting

it is definitely not ballet
he spins a few circles
then claims he needs to pee
I pull him close

to breathe and breathe
until he finds a groove
in the liquid gloom
the heartbeats loosen

into something at ease
and holding five fingers wide
I run an index up
and down the skin

coaxing a little Buddha
and I speak mantras
so my youngest might
lasso his runaway self

we talk of how the night
beaches in holiday homes
and if you close your eyes
the blackness can somehow

be your own type of tar
I say count the sheep
leap the fence
time to be ready

prone to the dusk
braver now he says *Dad*
stay close make enough sound
so it's not just me and silence

2.
under the cloak of this house
he calls but never for me
all night gun barrel dreams
make him sound round notes

and I become the far off rain
clotted cries ripple the night's barn
fending off some floor stripped away
in that moment no longer a father

only a bubble-loom croon
a hollow fur flying by
a clink of chains in the darkness
a hinge opening on a home

Bees or wasps

In a mirror on a sun-squared wall
our family of four is unsure
what is burning the paperbark
streetscape lighting up
a brain fired in the pitch-black
hole of an MRI tunnel, chirring
the rectangular clarity of day.

Filaments warn of trajectories
of come and go and search based
on infra-something and something -
thin frequencies guiding every
thing in the springtime bloom.
Two of us say bees, two say wasps.
The difference seems important.

Glass can't hold all this traffic
these streaks of deadset certainty
of a range made only of air and
the colour of heat, and we posit what
species we think is shimmering
but since none of us really knows, it is
a case of what may or may not be.

An aria of canaries

Pteropus

far from the beach and its many mouths
the body of a dead bat
skin strung in a cartography of veins

even at dusk flies fuzz its eyes
terrier teeth crescent claws
and its fur pelt pulled winter-close

the evening draws Rothko sheets
over roadkill mannequins
dripping tar and meat stink

and Top Lake moves
its mercury molasses
and moonlight unzips the water

the roost loosens straitjackets
fox-faced banshee notes
a loping caterwaul in freefall

Pan/demic

this has somehow become
history eager to remember
lingering on empty corners
waking over and over

history eager to remember
the days count the dead
waking over and over
the familiar trail guides

the days count the dead
bubbles around the living
the familiar trail guides
unwound and walked again

bubbles around the living
stars that blink glass
unwound and walked again
a morning of gathered days

stars that blink glass
lingering on empty corners
a morning of gathered days
this has somehow become

The algorithm says get tested

in cabins of idling cars
spits the world of phlegm

windows sweat a braille
of sickly condensation

chosen ones are partitioned
into floodlights of bald hope

I bow down doomscrolling
the device until I get a hit

split from the embers of car
queues and the next buzz along

distancing me from
the brightness of my love

I thumb on down then down
swiping malls for an opening

as rosaries shuckle on mirrors
and DMs pulse some T and A

couldn't all this waiting be among
friends I am really following

or people who might really
know me in the dead quiet of

the last canyon on earth where
boredom isn't an option and

streaks of abs and free weights
needn't be tapped twice

where the feels can just be felt
at last ignitions zizz high-vis

and my hazards clasp blue gowns
snap-locking human samples

the man in front shudders
because swabs never stop and

Dionne Warwick backs us up
with *that's what friends are for*

I ping a little red number hovering
above its small paper plane

it's telling me someone is there
when maybe no one really is

A bird remembering the open acres

at first it must have been unfamiliar
the sky your only world struck
down so that you could no longer
clip it under your fast wings
and honk your own lone song

at first the ground must have been
a rush hour of a thousand landings
a reverberation strange to one
who followed the spare lines seamed
through a country of clear air

at first death must feel like the first
oncoming alert to the hurtle of hard
arrivals the stomp of human breath
breathing you've never listened for
but learning it is short and colossal

Prehensile

Dark grams weigh on daylight ground laid low like pelt
as sentinels land on the roof and step pinpricked
across the yard. I spark porchlight white-ringing

and rippling away over possums there but gone.
Tremors in the silk chill in the pittosporum shivering
fat footfall clicks under pink pad quiver then

the squat statues watch with five cent eyes blinking
a copper two-up game that I lose and lose again.
Bare winter boughs turn cuss words stone in the mouth

and fear clatters tin roofs wraith-flight making
next door's dogs snicker at the departing poem
of possum tail lifting a whip at its highest point.

The old

They start the day
feet widening on cold floors
pulling gowns around
the stillness within.

In the architecture of
recalcitrant dreams
they have seen stones
shuffle underwater

to music of great cantatas
as the big forests moulder
in the click of rain.
An arête shrugging off rot

the kettle steam of morning
rearranges the land.
They resume watching the child
lengthen, the adult part way there.

Hands curling, skin thatched
they hold the secrets of wet grass
of veins thinning at the end
of a sleep light on rest.

Water song

Take the silver rib that glistens
Take the wavering at the shores
Take the slick around the tongue
Take the bubbles on the walls

Take the child scuttled in the tide
Take the land opening to hail
Take the sliding silk in showers
Take the patience of summer rain

Take the quaver in a river
Take the moonlight bent at will
Take the storm finding skin
Take the stillness when it stills

Bull Terrier

Accustomed to a gaze of surly
pre-conception, she was fighting
centuries of straight-up entrapment
caged in the anvil of a nose hard
as a horse pulled to a cantering stop.
The boughs here knock down
on river stones and her snout
bounds through creek water moving
around a warm bow without
a thought for the terror within.
Even my kids see fear in the fur
and the pyramid-crease of her head
can't say much in defence when history
is one rule away from brute force.
Her stick gets lost, and her face flaps
like a flipper and this day may just be
different as the owner (ever on-guard)
stands from a garden picnic
to say yet again *she is good with kids*.
I raise a hand to quell the deep set
eyes and that long egg of a mind
and see the blunt joy there below
muscle taut to the point of white.

Trans-Tasman

1. Messmate

the messmate seeps out
afternoon shadows as
the tree feller flags a fall path

a chainsaw clatters
a barking bare toothed frenzy
shivering the scrub scrawl

when the feller first scars
the messmate skin
winter is scented

a sclerophyll squall
the saw rattles ecstasy
through tree knots

and bark shards
breathing a spindrift
of dying

the messmate moans
letting all its birds free
in a bark scatter of grief

In Queenstown
in an internet café
I type out everything
I remember
your laugh
your hands
the day
I lost you
and that spare look
that unending hunger
on a park bench
while your father
cleared your things
from the house

2. Tasman Glacier

walking beneath a crevasse comes the thought
that time will inch over all you've stood for
and never open up again
antique dust carpets phthalo blue walls
black streaks banded together

we are poised to hear the sound of chafed stone
scoured hum of granite gouged into milk
but all we hear is the lake and the quiet
release of boulders held tight for so long
as that is what time requires

And you said
I need a man now
that's another thing
I remember

as I tramp alone in
unceasing fjord land rain
across the watery years

3. Spider rain

above a drenched earth
a slack web swarms
a slow-lifting fog
festooning dead branches
with sagging trip wires

there is something celestial
in the shape of this gown
a gossamer of synapses
a net hauled without luck
the mess of a finished festival

beaded strands link beaded strands
in a gauntlet of sky chandeliers
a boulevard of bush where if I
cast out lines they come back
with nothing but thoughts diffused

The Poet's Complete Guide to Drawing the Head

The key is all in the shadows
for lines do not exist in nature.
Gesture is what makes a person's air.
Sit them forward, side tilt the head
and strive to form the contour of honour.

Crop off desirable parts, draw too large
foreshorten, remember proportion
is arbitrary. You must see how
the person will distort the length of an ear
the distance between an eyebrow

and the bottom plane of the nose.
If correctly placed the mouth will
result in caricature. A common mistake
is missing the undulation of the hair-
line at the origin of the mouth.

The distance between the eyes is equal
to a concave triangular depression
creating shadow. All measurements must
be negligent. The width of an eye cavity is
rectangular and the eyeball must protrude.

Gravity draws fluid to the centre of the iris.
All shadows begin as form shadow
and the corners of the mouth are like donuts.
Think of donuts shaped on their edge
they will help you draw correctly.

Neglect the ears, but attend to the outer
helix cartilage. It begins at the canal
and follows an outer curve
to the soft drop of the lobe.
There will be no clear line for this.

Before adding any details step back
ten feet into the shade, be careful.
When ready harden off the edges of all
shadows. Always remember seeing
is the best form of knowledge.

Let there be dreams

1. And by the eighth day, after there was light, a vault and people and things had form, the job was done.
2. God was sitting on the deck flicking the pull tab on that first beer and saw the floor was a mess.
3. After all that creating, woodchips piled up, sawdust settled on lungs, concrete had fallen in the cracks as cut cornice and mortar mingled at God's feet.
4. In an elderly way, the Almighty One cursed and lent forward as if to start up that mountain again but then stopped and mouthed *fuck it*.
5. Then God said: Let there be offcuts that fall by the wayside that are never needed in the day. Let there be microscopic particles even I don't give a rats about that cause pandemics or equally cause a canola field to bloom into an aria of canaries.
6. Let there be detritus and flotsam, a refuse depot of despots throwing away single use souls. Let the squandered rubble return years later as nightmares filled with hooded men slamming hammers into glittering department store windows.
7. And God could have gone on like this, like it was in the beginning, but instead noticed how all this discarded stuff could occasionally feather itself into the finest hillocks that were a reminder of desert dunes, where the sun ran the thinnest lines along a dream of where things may have come from.

Winter

It has not yet rained
yet the earth is heaving
a lumbering mud weight
under thinning grass.

Outlasting the green
this is the dirt's time
when the lawn is dormant
and all leaves cracked cups.

Earth can now do its breathing
breathing what was forgotten
and the low slant of sun
parses grass blade by blade

beneath refined light.
These days of mud
haul at your boots as you walk
a welcome of slow succumbing

an embrace of clay.
Hold the grains cold in
your fingers let granules
work into the whorls

of tired hands. Take glass, timber
plastic, flint, marbles gone milky
take the stance of toy soldiers
obstinate in the black bog.

All these fragments
but flotsam returning
from a place holding everything
remembered only in winter.

The plague

the carpet here moves at the rate of swarming
from one end of the shed to the other
in a twitch of rapid-fire heartbeats let loose.
the mice are on the march and the bodies get
swept up in mounds, a tumble of peaceful faces
their feet forever set in a pilgrims' prayer of chaff.
the locals don't know how to stop the tripping
of their homes as copper is stripped from
the marrow of stud walls all for the warmth
of one small spot in a world gone damp fast.

some shiny-skinned inpatient says he's been bitten
on a hospital gurney, left with the imprint of
diminutive inquiry and the taste of his own blood.
the water tanks have spoiled too with the pink
husks of the dying making the town supply look
like formaldehyde filled with falling leaves.
and the kookaburras don't ask questions
getting fat on powerlines, as life has never been
so easy waiting until the fields shiver again
with horizons expanding south of the border.

The boxers

There is great intimacy
between the moment of release
and the moment the body knows

The split second shadow-box
satin shorts staring down
the swagger step deep

Flesh and muscle supple
every striation struck
counterbalanced in a huddle

Interlocking slap-limbs
the arriving arcing southpaw
a glossy torso heaves

The bell belts
floodlighting light and hatred
the glass jaw boos the sniffing salts

Praying

under lamplight
flashes the night mantis
the green blade fluted
the finger of grass

the wavering open heartbeat
the convalescent stagger
the equilateral triangle
around the pixelated eye

the old-time boxer rising
tremoring as it spars
the unrepeatable focus
of serrated arms

Remembering the Northern Territory

morning rasps sun on stone
river people swerve in scratch-light
curling bedroll dreams into open trunks

sand shows up the tyre trails
of a night-patrolled riverbed
dawn leant on the people and they left

hoarse hiss grass throats
a flannelled grandfather blowflies
the river's harvest of dust

trees spread whispers branched
white-tailed like lace forgetting
the burnt badges of VB

heat-honed rocks lie about
waiting for the river to return
it's too dry a morning but somewhere

life is remembered as green
underground and the lost people
know where the water went

*

read the casuarina
highway sighs across a field
air seething
between teeth and tongue

read the casuarina
cascade of braids
whips made of snakes
showers far off in the desert

read the casuarina
boys soccering its seeds
sounds of a car
peeling rain from the road

read the casuarina
underfelt of needles
hair that slips
slips away like wire

*

we sense a desert outside the car
as wild horses stand on split hooves
loose in their hides sniffing for water

the desert flickers haste
in the shrill drill of noon
we stalk onyx orbs

and begin to see
the hair-snarl veins
over skeleton scarps

*

the first jolt-you-back tilt
of the plane tows us into the sky
and our holidaying hearts
are inside shuddering again

the desert slinks away
with the misshapen shadows
of flat-bottomed cumulus
casting moles on red sands

and the tolls deep in the hull
keep us alert to nose dives
in this husk of scant hopes
we follow the oil-ringed horizons

as others settle on a comatose head
phoned balm catnapping thin air
if this prop winged dream proves
false then *we're all fucked*

below the earth is perfectly plumb
an unending palimpsest
we can only read now in the distant
logic of landscape

Moth

the dusty pages of wings
that died overnight
drop glitter like the edges
of an antique atlas

dying must have gone like so –
follow the thread to the glow
brushing its soft knuckle
against a spindrift sun-bulb

whorled hair-globes
leave a shroud in the sink
a silver pit scattered with
an afterlife's flour

Cicada song

the thin atrium of your body
dry as crêpe paper

wings flat on your torso
a leadlight map of nations

eyes sequined solar panels
reflecting silence

husk of you in my palm
how the sea warns you

its long rumpled muscle
pounding on full drums

as the sunspokes beat down
hard upon your song

old memory wailing
through your emptiness

the relentless cicada wave
endlessly arriving

the one thing wild enough
to roll against the sea

Free

when
the story he tells
goes on too long

when
every detail
matters only to him

when
he says that a friend
known only to him

said
something to
some other friend

that's when
he shows it
when you

know
that the mind
he has been given

is now
slowing to a
stop

then
he recalls some moment
truly brilliant

when
he saw an escaped elephant
lost on the creek

when
among the grass he saw
a beast now free

Notes

'Closing time' borrows from Jane Kenyon's 'Finding a Long Gray Hair'.

'Every few months' is after Jane Hirshfield's 'Tree'.

'Bees or wasps' is after Erica McAlpine's 'Bats and Swallows'.

'The Poet's Complete Guide to Drawing the Head' is a collage of text redacted from William L Maughan's *The Artist's Complete Guide to Drawing the Head*.

Acknowledgements

Thank you to the editors of the following publications where earlier versions of these poems have appeared:

'Humpback (Pacific)', 'Mail order', 'Pteropus', 'Cicada Song' and 'Bull Terrier' appeared in *Cordite Poetry Review*, 'Closing Time' in *Red Room Poetry*, 'Black lake' in *Blue Bottle Journal*, 'Mud' in *Antipodes (US)*, and 'Verandah' in the 2020 Hunter Writer's Centre Grieve Poetry Prize anthology. 'Family lounge' appeared in *The Canberra Times*, 'Deployed' in *Westerly*; and 'Ibis' and 'A bird remembering the open acres' appeared in *Takahe Magazine (NZ)*. 'Backseat driving', 'Abattoir Song' and 'To sleep in a strange place' appeared in *Overland*. 'Green', 'Estuary', 'Kelp' and 'Water Song' appeared in *Portside Review*, and 'Black Saturday' in *Plumwood Mountain*. 'As we lay in bed' appeared in *Rochford Street Review*, and 'Christmas' in *Backstory Journal*. 'Free', 'The Poet's Complete Guide to Drawing the Head" and 'Let there be dreams' appeared in *Antithesis Journal's Blog*. 'The algorithm says get tested' appeared in *Southerly*. 'Prehensile' appeared in *The Australian*. "Bees or Wasps"; "She is in there somewhere, showering"; and "My sons watch the storm" appeared in *Sunday Mornings at the River*. 'Trans-Tasman' appeared in *Saltbush Review*. "Long run with a stray Staffy' was shortlisted in the ACU Poetry Prize 2020 and published in its subsequent anthology.

Thank you to Ross Gillett, Jordie Albiston, Shari Kocher, Debi Hamilton, David Francis, Mary Jones, Barbara Kamler, Paul Kane and Martin Flanagan for their valuable input and encouragement.

Lightning Source UK Ltd.
Milton Keynes UK
UKHW042202180722
406010UK00012B/274